CITIZEN OF METROPOLIS

by

Christine Howey

Citizen of Metropolis

Poems ©2018 by Christine Howey
exactchangetheplay.com
all rights reserved by the author

Front cover art ©2018 by Steven B. Smith
walkingthinice.com / agentofchaos.com

Crisis Chronicles #99
ISBN: 978-1-64092-971-5
1st edition, 1st printing, 125 copies

Published 2 August 2018 by
Crisis Chronicles Press
John Burroughs, editor
3431 George Avenue
Parma, Ohio 44134 USA

crisischronicles.com
ccpress.blogspot.com
facebook.com/crisischroniclespress

Acknowledgments

Beowulf at Breakfast — *Star*Line* (Autumn 2013)
Taking Bryn, Age 7, to MOMA — *Poetry 4 Food - FourPlay #6* (2012, Writing Knights)

Contents

Citizen of Metropolis
I Don't Like This Title
Things That Make Me Sit
Satisfaction
Rock-A-Bye Baby
One Second
My Muse Eats Cheetos
Destination Vacation
Meals
Losing It at Age 73
Edward Hopper, Motivational Speaker
An Evening Out
Beowulf at Breakfast
I Want to Write a Poem with the Wires Showing
My Grandson on a Sled
Taking Bryn, Age 7, to MOMA
There are Parts of My Body I No Longer Encourage
      People to Handle Freely
Weather Report
William Randolph Hearst, Diving Alone, San Simeon

Citizen of Metropolis

I always wanted to be a citizen of Metropolis.
Every other kid wanted to be Superman.
Not me.
I wanted to be a citizen.

Falling backwards through the sky, secure
in the knowledge that Superman would
appear and save me.

(Not hero worship. I had no courage for that.
Not a come on. I had no interest in men, super
or otherwise.)

I just wanted to be seen, as a person.
Pushed from a tall building or tripping
face-first off a bus.
A person of Metropolis.
Worthy of being saved.
Just because I'm there, in the air.

I Don't Like This Title

And I don't much care for this line
break. Or this one.

As for the first stanza, it leaves me
feeling wan and slightly dissipated.

Then again, the second stanza seems
brighter to me, more fulsome.

But the third stanza plunges me
deep into the depths of dank ennui.

Oh, God! Rhyming in the fourth stanza? Really?
Just redo those last two lines before you go any further.

Now, I sense the end approaching, and it fills
me with dread, and yet, a touch of joy.

To be ended is a good thing. Not so good
as a Miles Davis solo, perhaps, but peaceful. Silent.

Things That Make Me Sit

Carl Sagan and then Neil deGrasse Tyson: a stellar televised one-two punch to my internal locator that places me at the correct coordinates in time and space, in the known universe. On the show *Cosmos*, the old one and the new one, Neil and Carl tell me what I see in this moment, in the sky at night, disappeared eons ago, telling me that this minute might warp through a time distillation, bouncing off dark stars and toss me down a gravity well. Yes, Sagan and deGrasse Tyson have done a number on me. Yes, it's the "trillions of billions" number, the one I can't conceive of even while strapped into their Ship of Imagination. It's the number of days leading to the next great extinction, it's the number of planets and stars that render Earth a tiny dot amidst the shoreless ocean of stars and planets, and me an infinitesimal dot lost on the vast expanse of that other tiny dot. Stunned by my own insignificance, I sit.

Then, clicking the remote, I see a commercial for The Clapper, the device that turns lamps on and off when you clap your hands. The commercial is a sure sign, like the Chia Pet, that it is the holiday season again. Another year has passed. It's been a whole year since I bought The Clapper. In the scope of universe time, a year is a fragile sliver of a millionth of a nanosecond. Making my life only a blink. Then again, two claps and the lamp goes on, two more claps and the lamp goes off. On and off. Empowered by the control I wield over my known universe, without even standing up, I proudly sit, The Clapper in hand.

Then I remember the scientific study that says you should never sit for very long because sitting, even for a couple hours, is like being a corpse, and if you sit even for a couple hours you will undo any good that your hour of Stairmaster exercise did earlier in the day. This thought exhausts me. Petrified by the damage done by anything other than constant standing, I sit.

—>

The way I look at it, if God didn't want us to sit, he would have made our knees bend the other way. And as Stephen Wright once asked, if our knees bent the other way, what would our chairs look like? I'm going to have to sit and think about that.

Satisfaction

Every stroke of the oblong block scraper
makes it a little bit better, plowing into blood
and gristle, little bits of gut curling up
the metal blades and falling onto the sawdust floor.

Four rows of scraper blades, flat at the tips
so they can dig and still advance across
the butcher's block, skimming dark crimson,
slick from fat after a day's cutting.

Ten blades in each of the four rows, making
surprisingly quick work of the blood bath,
the red disappearing more and more with each
push until only a maroon dot remains.

I doubt I will ever have a job so gratifying, every
gesture rewarded. Then, a final swipe to render
the wood dry, smooth and free from stain,
ready for tomorrow's onslaught.

Rock-A-Bye Baby

Hey there, new moms and dads, I know what you're thinking. You're thinking, sure, it's nice to rock our baby in his or her cradle right here by my side on the porch or in the living room. But it just doesn't seem like enough, not when there's a lullaby that paints a much more interesting alternative.

Yes, for years parents have been longing to give their infants the experience so often sung to them at bedtime: "Rock-a-bye baby in the treetop." It was always a lovely, entrancing image, but who thought it would ever be possible? Well, now it IS possible with the Treetop Baby Cradle. Our senior cradle engineers have spent years developing and testing this remarkable product, and thanks to our exclusive Twig'n'Branch™ cradle shell design, it will adapt to virtually any treetop you can find. Plus, you can be assured that when the wind blows, this cradle will rock! Made of solid Peruvian Jatoba cherry wood, the Treetop Baby Cradle is guaranteed to rock even in the wispiest puff of air, thanks to our patented Breeze-Touch™ Teflon-coated slider arms.

Just place the baby into the cradle and then position the cradle in the treetop of your choice, the higher the better! Then you can relax down below on the patio and watch as your little tyke rocks back and forth in the winds aloft, safe from any predators on the ground. Think of the glorious hours you will spend as your baby enjoys a peerless view of the blue sky, white clouds drifting by, and the occasional curious crow or squirrel that will likely perch on the cradle headboard. What baby could not fall into blissful sleep in such a setting?

Caution
Treetop Baby Cradle, Inc. does not assume responsibility for any injuries incurred during the placement or retrieval of the Cradle. NOTE: If a bough breaks the Cradle will fall, and down will come baby, Cradle and all.

One Second

For some reason,
it stops but I just keep
on moving. Let me explain.
Time stops. I think it's frozen,
at first, but it's not. There is some
slight motion, and then I discover that
the motion repeats itself, for one second:
a drop of tea moving a fraction of an inch down
the lip of my cup, over and over. Weirdly I know I
can get up and walk around. But I don't. I keep looking
at the little curl of tea on the white cup, slide down, slide
down. Such a luxury, to live inside this one moment, this one
tiny second. I have the time now to look outside and see a
squirrel begin to twitch his flowing tail, and begin again,
and again. And then I think I must be, by definition,
immortal. If this one second keeps repeating,
somehow keeps repeating, I will never die
because I am alive in this moment that
never goes away. This second is all
there is, all there will ever be.
I need to look again at it,
the curl of tan tea, the
taut brown squirrel.

So little to see, so much time to see it in.

My Muse Eats Cheetos

I don't know if your muse is a lovely young woman dressed in a flowing tunic and strumming a harp but mine is a 13-year-old girl with two nose piercings and holding a giant bag of Cheetos. I mean, she only eats Cheetos. When I come up with an idea for a poem, she rolls her eyes. For instance, when I think of writing about flowers she rolls her eyes, crunching on a Cheeto. So I say, you have a better idea? And she says, it's your job to come up with ideas. And I say, that's not what I read, I read that muses offer inspiration. And she says, how's this for inspiration? And she stuffs her mouth full of Cheetos. So I send her to her room, but she doesn't go anywhere because she doesn't have a room because she is a muse and she lives inside my head where she will always be 13 years old and dissatisfied with everything I write. So one time, to get on her good side, I read her a poem I wrote about Cheetos, a lyrical, soaring tribute to those curled bits of processed chemicals that pass for an edible food snack. And when I was finished,

    her face
            glowed lush and shimmery as if loomed
                    from the dreams of pampered kittens,
        her eyes were plump blue grapes
                        misted with ancient dew,
    her arms reached out through
            walls and around the world as she embraced me,
        smiling a smile
    so comely, so beauteous it made two passing butterflies
                    commit suicide from envy.

That was a nice moment, but it passed. She's here now, fingertips and lips stained neon orange, laying on the couch with her legs slung over the back, spilling Cheetos onto the floor. She snorts at my idea of a poem about alien invaders, saying that it sounds really stupid. I nod, then I start writing it. I take my inspiration wherever I can get it.

Destination Vacation

Their ships arrive three times every year, early on Saturday morning on the first full weekend after the last day of winter, spring and fall. We're used to it now, those copper-colored shapes shimmering in the sky as far as the eye can see. The airline industry knows not to schedule flights during that time, after the horrendous disasters that occurred the first time, airplanes crashing into those towering, gleaming spaceships.

Now, the whole world knows that the visitors will disembark from their vehicles in their usual, awkward manner and then move amongst us. No reason to hide, since we know these beings are benign if we don't strike out at them. Despite their horrific appearance, we all try to smile and go about our business. Our old conceptions of what extraterrestrials might look like—kind of like us but with bulbous heads and almond-shaped eyes—have been replaced with this stomach-churning reality. We were so naïve.

Since they look like they do, it's hard to tell the parents from the children, but we do realize that these are families. Thousands of them, spread out all across the globe, on holiday. They go where they want, we know now to leave all doors open. That means every door, we learned that the hard way. When we are active, doing our daily chores, the visitors near us remain motionless, looking at us, we have to assume, since they have nothing resembling eyes. But when we stop doing something to rest or nap, they move on and are soon replaced by others.

They never sleep while they're here, you can hear them moving in the night, even on the carpet past your bed. They take what they want, many things, odd things. A small sampling: white and brown shoes—strange, since they have nothing resembling feet—extension cords, nutcrackers. It's smart to have a few of each on hand.

—>

It seems we are their theme park, their "Renaissance Faire" or Frontierland at Disneyland, a quaint place to visit to see what life might have been like for the visitors if they hadn't been so fortunate to turn out as they did, when they did. Then, late Sunday night, they're gone. They are neat, nothing left behind, no trails of slime like you might expect, given their appearance. Just a faint odor of camphor and a piercing whistle that lasts exactly a week, then disappears.

Meals

There are too many of them, every day, multiple times a day.
And then you have to shop for them.
And then you have to go back to the grocery store and get what you forgot.
And then you have to answer questions about what you're making for the next meal.
And then you have to say, "No, we're not having that, we had that yesterday."
And then you have to say, "Well, if you don't like it, you don't have to eat."
And then you wonder why you didn't marry someone more mature.
And then you eat.
And then you clean up.
And then you relax until you realize you have to do it all over again in five hours.
And then you think, "What if I didn't do this, didn't recognize the existence of 'meals?'"
And then you decide not to prepare the next one.
And then you picture him asking, "Is it ready yet?"
And then you picture you responding, "Is what ready yet?"
And then he says something and then you say something and that goes back and forth for a while and then you hear the back door slam.
And then you settle into the couch with a half-gallon carton of Ben & Jerry's Super Fudge Chunk ice cream, one spoon, and a can of Reddi-Wip.
And then you think about when he will find you later, passed out with the collapsed carton of ice cream on your stomach and the empty Reddi-Wip can in your fist.
And then you stick the nozzle into your mouth.

Losing It at Age 73

If I could have all the time back that I've spent looking for things that I can't find, I'd be 24 years old right now. I don't say this to complain. My futile searches—for my watch, my shoes (no, not those, the other ones), my key to the porch door—have their upside. I get to see a lot of the rooms in my house that I don't normally visit. I don't need to join an exercise club, all I have to do is try to leave the house once or twice a day and then try to find everything I need, pounding up and down the stairs, and then again, and again. It's good lung exercise, as I stride from room to room screaming, "Where IS it? I am such an IDIOT! Where did I PUT it?" The search is often elongated when I wind up in a room and forget what I'm looking for. "Why did I come UP here?!" Then I have to retrace my steps to remember what I was looking for before I can continue looking for the thing I can't remember.

And I can lose things in record time. I'm talking Guinness Book of Records record time. Okay: I'm writing a check, I tear it out of the checkbook, I look up at my laptop when it dings to see who sent me an email, I look down and the check is gone? Who else can do that? Houdini? So I look, and look. Screaming. Finally, I find the check tucked into my address book. First of all, who still has an address book in this digital age? I do, so I can lose things in it! Second of all, why did I absent-mindedly put the check into the address book? Or did it just land there accidentally? Third of all, why am I still writing checks in this digital age?

Then there are the things I lose intentionally. Well, not intentionally, but with great care and forethought. Okay, I have this sheet of instructions for my new phone answering machine and I know I have to put it somewhere safe so I can find it because my phone answering machines never work right. So I look around and spy a tiny little drawer in an obscure corner of the antique secretary desk, a drawer that I never use. That's the perfect place for something this important! So I carefully fold up that sheet and place it carefully into that little drawer and, of course, I never see that sheet of instructions again, ever, because I NEVER USE

THAT DRAWER. Not only that, why am I using a phone answering machine in this digital age?

Just today I couldn't find my scarf (no, not that one, the other one), my gloves (no, the black ones), my mints (I never found them), and my car keys (they were in the pocket of the other winter coat, the one I never wear. Except when I do).

But, you know, I feel quite fit, and my lungs are in dandy shape.

Edward Hopper, Motivational Speaker

Hi, everybody! Before I begin, a funny story. One time, I'm sitting in an empty hotel room watching the late-afternoon sun cut a shadow like a black stab across the carpet and onto the wall. Across the street in a diner, a young woman rests her elbows on the counter, looking at a narrow slice of cherry pie in a clear plastic display case, her meatloaf growing cold on a blue plate. One door away, an ordinary man in a soft cloth hat stands on a threshold, staring into the deserted street. Above him, on the second floor, a no-longer-young man sits, focused on a blank sheet of paper on his clean desk. All around him are large windows he has not looked out of, ever. And in a town similar to this one, up the road, a 53-year-old woman with brown hair stands naked, head down, in a pool of light in a furnished room she rents by the week. But seriously, shoot for the moon.

An Evening Out

I sit at the bar.

What'll you have?

I'm Dan.

Hi Dan, what'll you have?

Bud.

A man sits next to me and orders Rolling Rock.

You drink that piss? Rolling Rock? I say to him.

He glares at me.

I shrug and laugh.

Did I hear you right? he says.

You heard me, jerk, I say, and turn away.

He slugs me sharp, quick, hard on the cheek.

I fall on the floor and the bartender takes me outside.

Get lost, he says.

It's always that way.

Beowulf at Breakfast

Hey, babe, your eggs are ready! Honey? How'd you sleep?

Too sore the anguish. Ettins and elves and evil spirits. The most baneful of burdens and bales of the night!

Another bad dream. Listen, I told you dragging the ram into bed with us was not a good idea. You want raisin toast?

A hot surge waiting of furious flame!

Don't be silly, the eggs are just a little warm. What's on tap for today, hon?

A scathing monster, dark ill-doer—

Just…stop. You know I'm tired of this whole Grendel thing. To begin with, you're never satisfied how I burnish your shield.

Harness gray and helmet grim, spears in multitude!

Yes. All of it. It's just too much for me to get ready. Plus, Sheila is coming over later and I have to bake my vole casserole.

With gripe alone I must front the fiend and fight for life, foe against foe!?

And you remember what Dr. Smith told you, that you're becoming a touch obsessive.

My blood-covered body he'll bear as prey, ruthless defile, devour, and destroy—

And a tad morbid, if you take my meaning. You know, the doc thinks all this alliteration is some sort of Tourette's thing. Did you answer me about the toast?

If death must take me as my life-blood reddens his lair in the fen, no further for me need'st food prepare!

A simple "No, thanks" would have sufficed. Have a nice day, sweetie. And take the trash bag to the curb on your way out, okay?

Thou gory sark, thou gilded swine-crest boar!

I heard that!

I Want to Write a Poem with the Wires Showing

I want the wires attached to bolts
that stick out from its sides
the wires wrapping around rough boards
braided with barbed wire that dig
into the wood leaving splinters.

I want nails pounded and bent
flattened against the wire with sharp
edges sticking out and rust,
chipped paint, smudges of black tar
asphalt, and ragged holes made

from sweaty hammer swings. I want
a poem that feels like keying
a car, I want to hear the sharp
squee of metal on metal. I want no
symmetry I want shapeless edges I

want wreckage on the page I want it
to be unreadable I want people to
know how it feels.

My Grandson on a Sled

A third of the way down the hill
Dashiell sits like all four-year-olds, planted
secure, a bean bag in snowpants,
eyes focused on the bottom of the hill,
waiting
as mom and dad try to analyze
why his sled isn't sliding
like the others.

Discs and toboggans fly down beside
him. But he waits with the strange
patience that sometimes, but rarely,
settles on a toddler. He seems so wise,
as snowflakes dot his eyelashes,
his eyesight swirling downhill,
sure that the thrill is about to start,
sure as the adults around him
that this will be a memorable moment.

Taking Bryn, Age 7, to MOMA

Curled in front of Andy's Marilyn
on the floor, re-routing
traffic around her.

An island of concentration
in a swirl of busy bodies.

Her eyes click from
icon to drawing pad
precisely, smoothly—
steel rails and ball bearings—
as she pencil sketches.

Other visitors stop and
take it in,
tapping a companion's shoulder if they
were facing elsewhere.

Smiles, nods, raised eyebrows.

We are all buoyed momentarily,
it seems,
to be in the company of creation
and inspiration.

Especially in one so small and
intense.

There Are Parts of My Body I No Longer Encourage People to Handle Freely

My kneecaps. Bony as they are, they work well and I sense that people with less than functional knees could be moved to violence—either from spite or from a desire to excise those parts of my body for their own nefarious use—by touching my kneecaps and detecting how well they operate.

My waist. This largely fictitious latitudinal band that circumnavigates my body should not be handled by any human other than a Board Certified mid-torso doctor or my dance partner in the Rumba class I no longer attend.

My eyelashes. No one should ever touch another person's eyelashes. Including mine.

My clavicle. Not because it is the only part of the anatomy that sounds like a quaint musical instrument, with the possible exception of the duodenum. But because my clavicle is powerfully sensuous and harbors the potentiality, at a single touch, of driving unsuspecting people delirious with lust. I regret that I cannot accept that kind of responsibility at this time.

Weather Report

Did you know that the weather segment is the most popular segment on the local news? Especially if the weather person is likable and feels like someone you could borrow a rake from if he or she lived next door. But most weather people on TV don't live next door to a person with a yard because they move around, so they live in rental apartments next to the station. They want to move to the next biggest market, and then the next, with hopes of being there at NBC when Al Roker finally keels over at his treadmill desk and the Today Show weather spot opens up. Until then, we watch the person who's telling us about the weather for tomorrow, even though we know the forecast is wrong. It's always wrong. But why do we get angry when it's wrong? We don't expect the news readers to predict the news tomorrow, or next week. Nor the sportscasters. They tell us what just happened, but that would not be sufficient for a full weather segment. Sure, they tell how the weather was today and then they show a state map with the high temperatures. "It was 86 degrees in Cleveland today, 85 in Canton and Painesville, 86 in Dayton, 81 in Berea." As if those slight temperature difference make any difference to us. "Hey honey, did you know it was five degrees cooler today in Berea?" "NOW you tell me. I would have been much more comfortable in Berea today, but now it's too late." Weather reports just sow discontent and malaise. Which is why weather forecasters smile a lot, trying to convince us they like us when we know they're just waiting for a better offer from Boston.

William Randolph Hearst, Diving Alone, San Simeon

He pulls all his heft—hard sauce
and cognac—onto the bending
board, positions his ramrod
stiff arms away from his head
little boy style, palm-to-palm.

When he springs to lift
off, looking down he plunges
towards dark blue tile, into night
sky of water-borne stars, buttery
swirls that gleam in his eye.

Breaching the surface,
a quick head swivel strafes
drops across dark ripples.
Then a flicker of movement.
A servant awaits poolside,

reminds him of constellations
he creates anew, illuminated
by hand, gold leaf sunk
in mosaic, the furled seaweed
and fluted shells, all specified.

Purchased. A world absent surprises
save those he has commissioned.
He receives his shoulder towel, steps
into leather slippers, and says quietly
that the fish below ought to be Pakistan

green, and made from smooth crystal
chips. Even against his weighty shuffle
he hears a pen nib scritch into memo
paper, somewhere in the darkness,
where no wishes go unanswered.

www.ingramcontent.com/pod-product-compliance
Lightning Source LLC
Chambersburg PA
CBHW071804040426
42446CB00012B/2713